Mastering Bitcoin

————— ❧❦❧❦❧❦❧ —————

How To Make Serious Money In 2018
Trading & Investing In Bitcoin

(Even If You're A Complete Beginner)

BOB HARRIS

Table of Contents

Introduction 1

Chapter 1:   Bitcoin Basics 3

Chapter 2:   Pros and Cons of Bitcoin 15

Chapter 3:   Bitcoin Wallets.......................................21

Chapter 4:   Make Money with Bitcoin......................27

Chapter 5:   The Future of Bitcoin.............................55

Conclusion 59

Introduction

Congratulations on downloading this book and thank you for doing so.

This book will teach you everything that you need to know about Bitcoin, as well as how you can turn it into a goldmine of profits. More and more people are interested in learning about Bitcoin for good reasons. As of the beginning of December 2017, the price of one bitcoin reached an all-time high of $10,000 USD.

The following chapters will walk you through the ins and outs of Bitcoin and reveal to you the effective ways to make money with it. If you want to buy your way to financial freedom, then this book is definitely the one for you.

Chapter 1 discusses the basics of Bitcoin. Before you invest your money, you should first have a good foundation and understanding of what Bitcoin is all about.

Chapter 2 talks about the pros and cons of using Bitcoin. Find out why so many people like to use Bitcoin, as well as the reasons why there are still some people who avoid it.

Chapter 3 explains what a Bitcoin wallet is all about. Learn about the different types of Bitcoin wallets, and know the one that will best suit your needs.

Chapter 4 reveals how you can make money with Bitcoin. Learn about Bitcoin mining, investing, and trading. This part of the book also discusses powerful strategies that you can use to make a decent profit.

Chapter 5 explores the possible future of Bitcoin. Find out why investing in Bitcoin today might just be the best investment decision that you can ever make.

There are plenty of books on this subject on the market, thanks again for choosing this one! Every effort was made to ensure it is full of as much useful information as possible. Please enjoy!

Chapter 1:

Bitcoin Basics

Introducing Bitcoin

Bitcoin is the most popular and successful cryptocurrency in the world. As of December 5, 2017, the price of 1 bitcoin is around $11,600 USD. What is a cryptocurrency? A cryptocurrency is a form of digital cash that is secured by cryptography. Just like any other cryptocurrency, Bitcoin does not have a physical existence. It is kept and stored electronically (online). Bitcoin functions as an effective substitute for money and a form of a payment system. Before we continue to discuss the features of Bitcoin, let us first take a look at how it all began.

Back in August of 2008, the domain name *bitcoin.org* was registered. In November of the same year, a paper entitled *Bitcoin: A Peer-to-Peer Electronic Cash System* was published in a cryptography mailing list, authored under the name Satoshi Nakamoto. In January of 2009, Bitcoin was finally launched in the market. It was also Nakamoto himself who mined the first block in the chain, known as the *genesis block*, for which he received a reward of 50 bitcoins.

It is worth noting that the name Satoshi Nakamoto is just a pseudonym. The true identity of Nakamoto remains unknown. He has long disappeared from the public view. There have been many theories and opinions as to his real identity. Some say that Satoshi Nakamoto is composed of a group of computer experts; others say that Nakamoto is one of the supporters of Bitcoin; there are even those who claim that Nakamoto is actually a woman. Despite all these opinions, to this day, no one can guarantee with 100% certainty the real person behind the name, Satoshi Nakamoto. Although the person or persons behind this legendary figure remain a mystery, the creation of Nakamoto has gained worldwide popularity and success, and that is the cryptocurrency, Bitcoin.

There were early supporters of Bitcoin. One of which is a programmer named, Hal Finney. There are those who believe that Nakamoto is Mr. Finney himself; however, Hal Finney denied this attribution. On the day Bitcoin was released, Hal Finney downloaded the software of Bitcoin. For doing so, he received 10 bitcoins from Satoshi Nakamoto. This is considered the very first Bitcoin transaction in history.

During the early stage of Bitcoin, its value was only subject to negotiation by the parties on the *bitcointalk* forum. Back then, Bitcoin did not have any significant value. In fact, there was a transaction where 10,000 bitcoins were paid for two pizzas. Today, a single bitcoin has a significant value amounting to more than $11,000 USD. What is more, its price keeps on increasing.

How the Bitcoin Protocol Works?

The Bitcoin protocol defines the procedures followed by every Bitcoin transaction from creation, validation, up to its final confirmation. Bitcoins are stored and spent using a Bitcoin wallet, and they are exchanged through a mechanism known as *Bitcoin transaction mechanism*. In order to have a better understanding of the Bitcoin protocol, you should first know the elements that govern a transaction. Every Bitcoin transaction contains the following information:

➢ Input

This refers to the source of the bitcoins that will be transferred to another. Before you can send bitcoins to another person, you must first have bitcoins in your own Bitcoin wallet; otherwise, there is nothing for you to send. For example, let us say that person X wants to send 2 bitcoins to Z. Before X can send 2 bitcoins to Z, X must first have 2 bitcoins in his wallet. This means that X must first receive bitcoins that are equal to or more than 2 bitcoins. This way, he will have enough bitcoins to send the said amount to Z. The input usually refers to the previous output where X is the receiver.

➢ Amount

Obviously, this refers to the amount of bitcoins that is involved in the transaction. In the given example, the amount involved is 2 bitcoins.

➢ Output

This refers to the receiver. In the example, this refers to the Bitcoin wallet address of person Z. Take note that in a Bitcoin transaction, bitcoins are sent between wallet addresses. The personal information of the persons involved remains private and confidential. It is also worth noting that a single Bitcoin wallet can generate multiple Bitcoin wallet addresses.

In terms of creation and validation of the Bitcoin process, the Bitcoin protocol broadcasts every transaction to all the nodes. The Bitcoin network is a public blockchain, and so all transactions are public and open to be viewed by everyone on the network. Each node in the Bitcoin system gathers the records and compiles them into a block. Every new transaction will also have to undergo validation before it can be added to the network. This is done by finding what is known as Proof of Work. This Proof of Work is a validation of current and past transactions by solving a mathematical puzzle. Once a node identifies a solution and confirms it, the record will then be added to the blockchain. Every node in the Bitcoin blockchain is connected to a previous block. This makes all the nodes over the Bitcoin network connected to one another.

How Bitcoin Is Different from Normal Currencies

Unlike normal currencies like the US dollar, Bitcoin is cryptocurrency. It has no physical existence but is held and stored online. It is also not considered as legal tender. This means that it is not something that a debtor can compel the creditor to accept payment.

Bitcoin has a decentralized network. This means that it is not regulated by central government or organization. This makes its system impossible to be manipulated or unduly influenced by anyone. Not even Satoshi Nakamoto can control the Bitcoin network.

Obviously, Bitcoin is not considered fiat money. Fiat money refers to the official currency of a state, such as the US dollar. For some people, this is considered a benefit since it means that Bitcoin is free from any manipulation that a higher authority can exercise over it, whether directly or indirectly. However, there are still some who think that the decentralized network of bitcoin is something to be cautious about. Unlike in banks where a person can enjoy some degree of insurance, there is no way to recover your bitcoins if somebody else is able to hack into your Bitcoin wallet and steal away your bitcoins.

Another thing that makes Bitcoin different from the normal currencies is the high volatility of the price of one bitcoin. On the one hand, the price of fiat money barely fluctuates. Normally, it only changes by a few cents on a day-to-day basis. On the other hand, the price of one bitcoin can fluctuate significantly within a short period of time. In fact, it is not uncommon for the price of bitcoin to fluctuate by more than 10% in a 24-hour timeline.

Understanding the Blockchain Technology

The blockchain technology is the technology behind Bitcoin. It is a decentralized and public ledger that has a high security. It is composed of a list of records known as blocks that are connected to each other and secured by cryptography. Cryptography refers to the process of securing information. It was used during the World Wars when it was important to ensure that the communication in the government and the army was kept private and confidential. It soon found its application in the world of cryptocurrency. Each block or record on the chain has a hash pointer which connects it to a previous block. The entire Bitcoin blockchain system is designed in such a way that the records would be almost impossible to modify or alter. Bitcoin blockchain is spread over a vast network of computers. This means that in order to change even a single transaction on the chain, all the users/computers on the network will have to give their consent.

The blockchain technology also has a strong security. There is a concept known as the 51% attack. According to this concept, the only way an attack against the blockchain can be successful is if the attack has at least 51% hash power. Considering that the Bitcoin blockchain is spread over a vast network of computers, such a kind of attack is virtually impossible. It is worth noting that this refers to the success of the attack, which means that an attack with less than 51% hash rate is still possible, but it will most likely fail.

The blockchain technology is the backbone of Bitcoin. Literally all Bitcoin transactions are recorded on the blockchain. Take note that when you use Bitcoin's blockchain, all confirmed transactions can no longer be canceled, withdrawn, or altered. This is an excellent preventive measure against fraud.

The blockchain technology is another revolution that is also gaining so much attention and interest. It has been discovered that the blockchain technology can be applied to things other than those related to cryptocurrency and financial services.

Bitcoin Core

This refers to the reference client of Bitcoin. It was originally published by Nakamoto simply as *Bitcoin*, but then it was renamed to Bitcoin Core in order to avoid confusion and differentiate it from the Bitcoin network or cryptocurrency itself. By changing the Bitcoin Core, the developers of Bitcoin can change the protocol. Take note that this does not give to the developers the power to change the records over the Bitcoin blockchain.

The Bitcoin Core has an engine for verifying transactions, and it also connects to the network as a complete node. The Bitcoin Core software validates the records that are included into the blockchain, which includes all transactions.

The first version of Bitcoin Core was Bitcoin 0.1. Back then, it could only support Windows. Over the years, developments and changes were made in order to make the Bitcoin client more responsive, as well as to enhance its quality. To this day, developments are continuously being made to Bitcoin Core.

Real World Use of Bitcoin

Being a substitute for money and a payment system, Bitcoin obviously has various uses. These days, many merchants accept the use of bitcoins as a medium of payment. In fact, even the giant computer software company, Microsoft, accepts bitcoins. The famous gaming platform, Steam, also accepts bitcoin. A company engaged in space tourism, Virgin Galactic, also accepts payments in bitcoins. Even Fiverr, Wikipedia, and Overstock, among others, accept bitcoins. In some states, you can now pay your electric and other household bills using Bitcoin. You can even book a hotel room and air-fare flight with Bitcoin. Although not considered as legal tender, many merchants and individuals turn to Bitcoin. Since Bitcoin has been proven to be highly lucrative investment, many people who invest in stocks, bonds, and realty, have switched to Bitcoin investing and trading. All that a merchant has to do is give you his or her Bitcoin wallet address, and you can send your payment in bitcoins at any time. Many people turn to Bitcoin because of the many benefits that they can enjoy as compared with using regular currency or fiat money. This will be discussed in detail in the following chapter.

It is noteworthy that the majority of the people these days who turn to Bitcoin do not really use it as a mode of payment. Of course, there are still some who do. After all, Bitcoin is a substitute for money. However, it cannot be denied that most people are drawn to bitcoin because of its high profit potential. Instead of investing in stocks where an increase of 15% in a year is already considered high, you can get even more than 100% increase by investing in Bitcoin within a short period of time. Indeed, many people are using bitcoins as way to financial freedom. Fortunately, there are many people who have already proven that this is not just a possibility but a reality.

Bitcoin is also used in online gambling. There are many Bitcoin gambling websites online. Making deposits and withdrawals with bitcoins are also much easier than using your bank's card. Most withdrawals can be completed almost instantly. In case of a huge withdrawal, it will most likely be completed within 24 hours.

As you can see, as long as people decide to use Bitcoin, then it will always have a use in the real world. The good news is that more and more individuals and businesses are switching to Bitcoin and accepting it as a medium of payment. Hence, you can rest assured that Bitcoin is not just a lucrative investment but is also very useful in the modern world.

Legality of using Bitcoin

The use of Bitcoin is generally legal. However, in a few states, such as in Ecuador, Kyrgyzstan, and Bolivia, the use of Bitcoin is completely outlawed. It should be noted that although Bitcoin itself is not regulated by any state, it does not mean that a state is without power to regulate its *use* within its territorial jurisdiction. After all, a state has a duty to serve and protect its people. Therefore, if a state believes that the use of a certain cryptocurrency is not good for its people, then it can take measures to regulate or completely restrict its use in the exercise of its police power. It is not hard to understand why there are still states that outlaw the use of Bitcoin, as well as states that impose strict regulations on the use of Bitcoin. Bitcoin users enjoy a high level of anonymity, which makes it prone to being abused. Due to the privacy and anonymity enjoyed by bitcoin users, it can be used in the commission of criminal activities, especially in money laundering.

If you analyze the trend of Bitcoin, you can somehow foresee that Bitcoin will most likely be accepted by all states. Years ago, Russia outlawed the use of Bitcoin. Today, Russia is one of the supporters of Bitcoin. There are also countries like Singapore that have not issued any regulation upon the use of Bitcoin and simply allow it to reach its maximum potential. To date, only a very few countries consider the use of Bitcoin to be illegal in their territory. But in most countries, including the United States of America, Canada, Europe, France, Japan, and others, the use of bitcoins is completely legal. Of course, some regulations may be expected. Nonetheless, the use of bitcoins is considered legal.

What are Altcoins?

Bitcoin is so successful that it is the leading standard of all cryptocurrencies. Although there are more than 900 cryptocurrencies that have already been created in the world, Bitcoin remains the number one cryptocurrency of all time. In fact, it has so well established itself that all other cryptocurrencies have been categorized as mere *altcoins* or *alternative coins*.

As can be expected, there is a continuous competition among the different cryptocurrencies. Although they all want to take the place of Bitcoin, it can be said that this is far from happening. The cryptocurrency that is next in rank after Bitcoin is known as Ethereum. As of December 2017, the price of 1 ether is only around $450 USD. As you can see, it has a long way to go to catch up with bitcoin. There are other notable altcoins, like Litecoin, Monero, Ripple, and Z-cash, among others.

In order to draw interest, altcoins add additional value. For example, the altcoin Ripple can help banks to make faster transactions. It is the only cryptocurrency that is in favor of banks and was made to actually help banks with their processes. The altcoin known as Litecoin is not new in the cryptocurrency market. It started in 2011 with an aim to be the better version of Bitcoin. Back then, people noticed that Bitcoin's speed of confirming transactions was quite slow, so Litecoin was made and designed in such a way that it can verify and complete transactions faster than bitcoin. Another noteworthy altcoin is Z-cash. Z-cash offers more private and secure transactions than Bitcoin. It allows what is referred to as "shielded transactions." When you use this shielded transaction feature, you will be allowed to hide not only the amount involved in a transaction but also the corresponding details of the sender and the receiver. This way you can rest assured that your transactions are completely private and confidential. There are many other altcoins in the market today. Gone are the days when a developer can just introduce a cryptocurrency and hope for the market to accept and use it. Today, if you introduce a new cryptocurrency, then you must package it in such a way that the market will see it as something useful and valuable.

Chapter 2:

Pros and Cons of Bitcoin

List of Pros

➢ Decentralized

The Bitcoin network is decentralized, which means that it is free from any form of manipulation. You get to exercise full authority and control over your bitcoins. You are also free to send and receive bitcoins as much as you want.

➢ Worldwide scope

The Bitcoin network is not limited to any geographical location. You can enjoy all the benefits that Bitcoin has to offer even if the other person is on the other side of the globe. If sending bitcoins, then all that you need is an Internet connection. If you are the receiver, then you do not even need to have computer or even Internet access. Just give your Bitcoin wallet address to the sender and wait for your bitcoins to arrive in your Bitcoin wallet.

➢ 24/7 service

Unlike banks that have opening and closing schedule, the Bitcoin network does not sleep. You can send and receive bitcoins even at 2AM. It is available at any time.

➢ Lower fee

This is one of the main advantages of using Bitcoin. When you use Bitcoin, you can remove the middleman and transact directly with another person. Needless to say, having a middleman means more cost. Instead of paying a middleman like a bank or a third-party service provider such as PayPal, you can make direct transactions using bitcoins. This does not only simplify the process but can significantly lower your expenses, especially if you intend to make numerous transactions. Although such additional costs that you may incur when you use a middleman may just be a small amount, said amount can turn into a significant amount in the long run.

➢ Convenient

Using bitcoins is very easy. Bitcoin transactions happen online and with just a few clicks of a mouse. In fact, you can make complete transactions simply by using your mobile phone. There is also no human interaction that is needed. Just go online and with just a few clicks, you can enter and complete bitcoin transactions.

➢ Quick transaction

Bitcoin transactions get verified and completed quickly. Most of the time, it will only take a few minutes for a transaction to complete. If you are willing to pay a small mining fee, then a transaction can be completed almost instantly. Hence, there is no more need for you to wait for days just for a certain check to clear. With bitcoins, you can enjoy ultra-fast transactions. What is more, it is very convenient to use.

➢ Increasing value

Of course, when it comes to using bitcoin, it is already common knowledge that it has a high value. Not only does it have a high value, but the price of one bitcoin is continuously increasing. In fact, this is the reason why many people these days want to start using and investing in bitcoins.

List of Cons

➢ Security risk

Although supporters of Bitcoin claim that Bitcoin is virtually invulnerable to any attack due to the 51‰ concept, there are still those who claim that it is still possible to be able to hack into Bitcoin's network even with less than 51‰ hash rate. The problem here is that Bitcoin nodes are interconnected. Therefore, if a bug or virus is able to penetrate even just a single node or block on the chain, then it will be able to affect the whole system. Although no one has yet been able to totally destroy Bitcoin's blockchain, the possibility that an attack against the blockchain may be successful cannot be discounted. There is also a possibility that an advanced bug or virus may be developed that will be able to infiltrate the blockchain's security. If this happens, then many Bitcoin accounts will most likely get compromised. And since the

Bitcoin blockchain is not regulated by any central authority, there would be no way to recover any lost or stolen bitcoins.

➤ Market risk

Admit the fact that it is difficult to predict how the market behaves and responds. Just because the market seems to patronize Bitcoin these days does not guarantee that it will continue to share the same preference after some time. For example, when China announced that it will close down all its local cryptocurrency exchanges, many investors panicked and pulled out their investments in Bitcoin. As a result, the price of Bitcoin dropped much lower than what was caused by China's decision to close down its local cryptocurrency exchanges. Also, contrary to what most people had thought of that time, Bitcoin was quickly able to recover from that incident. As an investor, you should realize that the market is outside of your control. However, how the market responds can significantly affect the price of bitcoins. The good news is that although how the market responds is outside of your control, you can study the market and most likely be able to predict the direction where it is heading.

➤ Legal risk

Although governments seem welcoming of Bitcoin and other cryptocurrencies, it does not mean that governments will no longer restrict or impose more restrictions on Bitcoin and other cryptocurrencies. Do not forget the fact that Bitcoin acts in direct competition with the official currency. Just imagine what will happen if the people all turn to Bitcoin. The price of fiat money will surely be affected. Due to the high demand for Bitcoin and low demand for the official currency, the price of the latter will definitely drop, and this is not good for the economy and the government. Hence, although governments seem to adapt a friendly attitude toward Bitcoin today, it does not mean that they will never impose other measures and restrictions on bitcoin in the future.

➢ High volatility

One of the main reasons why there are investors who do not want to invest in Bitcoin is because of its highly volatile nature. When you say that something has a high volatility, it means that its price rises or falls significantly and quickly within a short period of time. There are many investors who do not like this kind if investment because it also means that the risk is usually higher than the normal, because it means that you can also lose your money quickly. However, it should be noted that it is also this high volatility of Bitcoin that makes it a lucrative investment. It is what allows it to get a 20% or even 150% increase in value within a short period of time. What is good about investing in Bitcoin is that despite its highly volatile nature, it has proven to be a really profitable investment. If you look at the trends, it is obvious that its price is constantly increasing. Of course, it is also subject to the usual fluctuation in price. But, if you look at its long-term behavior, it cannot be denied that it is, indeed, a very profitable investment.

➢ Requires high-quality input

The Bitcoin blockchain system is destined in a way that the records should no longer be subject to any changes. Hence, all information sent over the blockchain must be of high quality. This means that you need to ensure that the information is correct. For example, if you are sending 10 bitcoins to person

B, then be sure to correctly input the amount of bitcoins to be sent, as well as the Bitcoin wallet address of B. Keep in mind that once a transaction has been confirmed, then there is no way of canceling or changing it.

Chapter 3:

Bitcoin Wallets

What is a Bitcoin Wallet?

Before you can even start to use bitcoins, you need to have a place where you can store them. The place where you keep your bitcoins is known as a Bitcoin wallet. When you use bitcoins, you need to understand that there are different kinds of Bitcoin wallets. The right wallet for you will depend on how you want to use bitcoins. Generally, Bitcoin wallets are categorized into two main types: hot wallet and cold wallet. A hot wallet is a kind of Bitcoin wallet that is stored online, while a cold wallet, which is also known as cold storage, is stored offline. Since hot wallets exist online, they are more convenient to use but are less secure since they are exposed to the Internet, which makes them possible targets for hackers and scammers online. Cold wallets are less convenient to use but are more secure since they are not exposed to the dangers of being discoverable on the web. Hot and cold wallets are further divided into more specific types of Bitcoin wallets. Let us take a look at them one by one.

Different Types of Bitcoin Wallets

➢ Web Wallet

A web wallet is the most common type of Bitcoin wallet. It is also referred to as an *online wallet.* This is the kind of wallet that you can create and use when you are connected to the Internet. You simply have to visit the website of your wallet provider and access your Bitcoin wallet online. A good example of a web wallet is the famous web wallet known as Coinbase. More than 60% of Bitcoin users prefer to use a web wallet more than any other kind of Bitcoin wallet. Although a web wallet is the best example of a hot wallet, it should be noted that web wallets these days have enhanced their security. Still, if you want a wallet with the highest security features, then a cold wallet is the one for you.

➢ Mobile wallet

A mobile wallet is another kind of hot wallet. It also functions like a web wallet with the additional feature that you can download it on your mobile device; hence, the name *mobile* wallet. Most web wallets are also mobile wallets. Again, an example is Coinbase. It has a website that you can access using your computer and yet it also has a mobile application that you can download on your mobile phone for free.

➢ Desktop wallet

This is a kind of cold wallet, also referred to as *computer wallet.* The reason is that it will allow you to store your bitcoins in a computer. Although usually called a *desktop* wallet, it can also be used to store bitcoins in a laptop. Hence, it is not limited to a mere desktop computer. If you decide to use a desktop wallet, then you should remember to only use one that has not been connected to the Internet. Again, exposure to the web would also expose it to bugs and viruses. If the computer that you intend to use as a desktop wallet has already been connected to the Internet, then you should first reformat it before using it as a desktop computer.

➢ Hardware wallet

A hardware wallet is another kind of cold storage. It also functions like a desktop wallet but instead of storing your bitcoins in a computer, you store them in a piece of hardware, such as a USB device. If you store your bitcoins in a hardware wallet, you should not use the said hardware for any other purpose except for storing bitcoins. For example, if you use a USB as a hardware wallet, you should no longer use the USB for storing other files. More importantly, do not connect the USB to a computer that is exposed to the Internet.

➢ Paper wallet

A paper wallet is another popular type of cold wallet. When you use a paper wallet, you store the public and private keys of your Bitcoin account on paper. They are printed on paper, and you simply keep the paper as if you were keeping paper money. Ideally, you should print several copies and be sure to keep them in a safe place separately. Hence, you can keep one copy in your real and physical wallet, another copy in your closet, etc.

So, which wallet type is for you? This will depend entirely on how you want to use bitcoins. If you are going to spend bitcoins on a regular basis, then a hot wallet is definitely the one for you. However, if you just want to invest in bitcoins where you just buy bitcoins and hold on to them until their price increases, then a cold wallet may the one for you. You are not limited to using just one Bitcoin wallet. Hence, you may want to use both hot and cold wallets, depending on your needs. Another option is to use different hot wallets at the same time.

Just to note: Although cold wallets tend to have higher security since they are not exposed to the Internet, there is still the risk that they may get lost, broken, or even stolen. If this happens, then it will be almost impossible to recover your bitcoins. Hence, even using cold wallets has risks.

Wallet Protection Tips

When you use Bitcoin, the protection of your wallet should be considered of primary importance. You need to ensure that your bitcoins are safe and secure. Here are important wallet protection tips that you should know:

➢ Use a strong password

Make sure that you are using a strong password. Your Bitcoin wallet password is your first and main line of defense against any attack against your account. A common mistake committed by so many people is to meet the minimum requirement of a website when making their password. Do not be satisfied with the site's minimum requirement. In order to have a strong password, you need to do much better than that. Hence, even if the required minimum for a password is only 6 characters long, make a password that is composed of more than 10 characters. Remember that the longer your password is, the better it is for the security of your account. You should also combine upper and lower case letters. Needless to say, you should never use passwords that can easily be predicted, such as your name, name of your pet, or your date of birth, etc. Make sure to use a password that people would not be able to guess correctly. A good piece of advice is to use a random string of letters and numbers. Just be sure not to forget about it. Another way to enhance your password is by using symbols and numbers. It is also a good practice to update (change) your password every now and then, especially when you feel like your account is being compromised.

➢ Always use a new wallet address

Take note that a Bitcoin wallet is different from a Bitcoin wallet address. A Bitcoin wallet can generate more than one Bitcoin wallet address. In a transaction, what will appear on the blockchain is the Bitcoin wallet address involved in a transaction. By using a new address for every new transaction, you can lower your exposure, which also means lower risk. Most Bitcoin wallets will allow you to generate a new Bitcoin wallet address instantly with just a click of a mouse. This is also free of charge.

➢ Check if the page is secure

Always check if the page is secure before you key in any sensitive informative, such as your wallet password. It is easy to do this: Simply look at the URL bar and check if there is a green padlock on the side. A green padlock is a sign that signifies that the current page is secure. You may also find the word "Secure." Never input your password or any other sensitive information if the page is not secure.

➢ Avoid public Wi-Fi's

Although there is nothing wrong with connecting to and using public Wi-Fi if you just want to surf the web, it is not safe to access your Bitcoin wallet using public Wi-Fi. It is not uncommon for hackers to take advantage of public Wi-Fi and use it to hack into the accounts of people who are connected to it. Simply stated, connecting to public Wi-Fi can lead you to be connected to a hacker who might be able to compromise your account. Therefore, never open or access your Bitcoin wallet when connected to public Wi-Fi.

➢ Use more than one bitcoin wallet

You are probably aware of the saying, "Do not put all your eggs in one basket." This is true when it comes to storing bitcoins, especially if you have lots of bitcoins. By using more than one wallet, you get to spread or minimize your risk. Hence, even if one of your wallets gets hacked, you will not lose all your bitcoins. Still, you should remember to only use trusted and secure Bitcoin wallets. It is not uncommon to find investors who use up to 7 different kinds of wallets. Of course, this will depend on how many bitcoins you have.

Chapter 4:

Make Money with Bitcoin

How to Buy, Sell, and Invest in Bitcoin

Although Bitcoin functions as a substitute for money, it cannot be denied that most of the people who possess bitcoins do so for the purpose of making money and not solely for the purpose of using it as a medium of exchange when buying things. In fact, if you look at how Bitcoin is being marketed, it appears more to be as a lucrative type of investment instead of being a mere substitute for money. So, how do you invest in bitcoin? When you invest in stocks, the first step to make a profit is for you to buy stocks. The same principle applies when you invest in bitcoins. The first step is to buy bitcoins.

➤ Buying bitcoins

Buying bitcoins is easy. There are some Bitcoin wallets like Coinbase and coins.ph that will allow you to buy bitcoins from the site itself. Another way is to join a trading platform like Bitfinex and purchase bitcoins (or other cryptocurrencies) on the platform. There are also sites like localbitcoins were people can buy and sell bitcoins. As you can see, there are many ways to buy bitcoins, and all it takes is for you to go online and make a few clicks. Needless to say, in order to buy bitcoins, you will have to spend real money, usually by using your VISA or Master card.

A common question asked by beginners is this: Can you buy bitcoins using PayPal? It is true that many people prefer to use PayPal when buying things online. The answer is *yes*. You can buy bitcoins using PayPal. There are some individuals and sites that may allow you to send the payment via PayPal. However, this is not the suggested method. The reason is that the process becomes very expensive. When you buy bitcoins using PayPal, a common suggestion is to use Virwox. Although this is possible and quite easy to do, the big drawback is that the process is very expensive. You may have to pay more than 25% of the market price. There are other sites that will allow you to buy bitcoins using PayPal, but then again the price that they offer is much more expensive than the actual market price.

Before buying any bitcoins, you should first look at the current market price. Of course, you can expect for the buy price to be higher than the selling price. After all, the seller also wants to make a profit. Unfortunately, there are many Bitcoin sellers online that sell bitcoins at a price that is obviously much higher than the actual market price. To be safe, it is advised that you purchase bitcoins from legitimate trading platforms or trusted Bitcoin wallets like Coinbase or coins.ph.

When buying bitcoins, proper timing is also important. Keep in mind that the price of Bitcoin can fluctuate significantly in a day. Before you make a buy order, it would help if you first research what is going on in the market. Do not forget the saying, "Buy when the price is low; sell when the price is high."

In order to make the most out of your money, try to buy bitcoins when its price is low. For example, if the price of bitcoin drops by 5% and you make a buy order at the said lower amount, then it is like getting a 5% discount for your purchase. If you are spending a significant amount of money, then even a 5% difference can be a big amount. Now, if you think that the price of Bitcoin will most likely increase today, then you can make a buy order right now without having to wait for its price to drop. Proper timing can save you money.

➤ Selling bitcoins

Buying bitcoins is just the first part of the process. If you want to realize your profit, then you need to turn those bitcoins into cash. The way to do this is by selling your bitcoins. So, how do you sell bitcoins? There are Bitcoin hot wallets that will allow you to sell bitcoins and have the money deposited into your bank account completely within the wallet's website. Again, good examples of this would be Coinbase and coins.ph. As already stated, localbitcoins is a place where individuals buy and sell bitcoins. You can create a free account and offer your bitcoins for sale. You then simply have to wait for someone to message you and purchase your bitcoins. A good way to sell bitcoins is by joining trading platforms like Bitfinex. You can easily and quickly sell your bitcoins and have the proceeds of the sale deposited into your linked bank account. If you want, you can also offer your bitcoins for sale on your website. This will work, especially if you have a website/blog that is about bitcoins.

When selling bitcoins, you should pay attention to the current market price of Bitcoin. You should look at and compare the selling price of Bitcoin as offered by different and legitimate brokers and websites. This way you will have a good idea on the fair price of selling your bitcoins. Of course, the price of Bitcoin continuously fluctuates, so you should expect for your selling price to also change over time.

➢ Investing in bitcoins

Investing in bitcoins is all about buying and selling bitcoins for profit. Once again, remember the saying: "Buy when the price is low, and sell when the price is high." A simple yet very effective way to invest in bitcoins is simply by buying bitcoins and just waiting for the price to increase. Once its price increases, you can then sell your bitcoins for a profit. This is, in fact, how many people who became a millionaire by investing in Bitcoin did it. The process is not complicated at all. It is all based upon the significantly increasing price of Bitcoin. The earlier that you invest in Bitcoin, the more that you can benefit from it.

Is it too late to invest in Bitcoin? The answer is *no*. Although the price of Bitcoin has already gotten quite high, it is still constantly increasing. In fact, according to many experts, the price of Bitcoin will continuously increase through 2018. Of course, just like any other cryptocurrency, it will still be subject to the usual fluctuations in price as it has always been. However, if you look at its long-term price direction, it cannot be denied that its value is constantly increasing without any issue. Considering that it is getting even more popular these days and that more people are getting interested in it, then you can also expect for more significant increases in the price of Bitcoin to take place. The Bitcoin revolution is simply unstoppable.

Investing vs. Trading Bitcoins

Is there a difference between investing in and trading bitcoins? It depends on how you view it. For the word Nazis out there, you can say that there are certain differences between trading and investing in bitcoin. On the one hand, trading usually refers to a more active approach. Also, when a person trades bitcoins, it usually includes trading other cryptocurrencies. It is also common for traders to open multiple trading positions in a single day. On the other hand, investing entails a passive approach. Normally, when a person invests in Bitcoin, it would only involve a buy and hold strategy where a person buys some bitcoins, waits for some time for the price of Bitcoin to increase, and then sell his bitcoins at a profit. If viewed from this perspective, then it may be said that trading and investing may be different from each other. However, it can also be said that investing and trading are the same or at least synonymous. After all, when you invest in Bitcoin, you will have to trade your money for Bitcoin and then vice versa. When you trade Bitcoin and other cryptocurrency, you will have to invest money to allow you to engage in such trading activities. From this perspective, investing and trading may mean the same thing. Regardless of how you want to call this activity or whether you view yourself as an investor or a trader, the important thing to take note of is how much money you make, if any.

Note: This book uses both terms synonymously.

Bitcoin Trading Strategies

➤ Fundamental analysis

Fundamental analysis is at the heart of every investment strategy. In fact, it is also referred to as the lifeblood of investment. So, what is fundamental analysis? As the name already implies, fundamental analysis deals with the fundamentals or the basics. Hence, it is the foundation of everything. After all, investing in or trading bitcoins is not a complicated matter. If you have a good understanding of the basics, then you can significantly increase your chances of making a nice profit.

When you use fundamental analysis, you should research and analyze the trend of Bitcoin, as well as the factors that affect its price, such the economy, technological developments, competition among the different cryptocurrencies in the market, government regulations that may affect Bitcoin, and market acceptance, among others. Indeed, financial analysis is the one that requires the most research and study. But, it is also a very effective strategy. The thing is that the more that you understand Bitcoin and the factors that have influence over it, the more easily you can predict its movement, which will allow you to make the right investment decision.

If you are a serious investor, then fundamental analysis is something that you should do every day. It should become a habit to you. Every day you are expected to be updated on what is going on in the world of Bitcoin and make your own analysis. The true application of fundamental analysis does not happen in a day; rather, it is something that you do every day and should be second nature to you. When it comes to investing, whether in Bitcoin or otherwise, the amount and quality of information that you have, as well as how you analyze the said information, matters a lot to the outcome of your investment.

➤ Technical analysis

If you are not fond of computing numbers and dealing with hard facts, then you might want to use technical analysis. When you use technical analysis, you will be analyzing graphs and charts that demonstrate the price behavior of Bitcoin. It will show you the past and present trend through its price movement. The idea behind this strategy is that all the factors that affect Bitcoin will have their final effect upon the price. Therefore, if you just analyze the price movement of Bitcoin, you also get to deal with all the many factors that affect Bitcoin's price. This like a simplified version of fundamental analysis and entails a more visual approach.

The key to this strategy is to learn to identify patterns. *But, wait a second — do patterns really exist?* The answer is *yes*. Patterns do exist. However, patterns also come and go, which means that you cannot always expect to see a pattern when you look at a graph. But, once you identify a certain pattern, then you should be able to take advantage of it. In fact, even a random generator can create patterns from time to time. A common mistake is to force yourself to see a pattern. Many people who use technical analysis think that since they have studied a certain graph for an hour, this already means that they should spot a pattern and make an investment right there and then. This approach is wrong. Again, patterns come and go. Therefore, if you do not see a pattern that you can take advantage of, the best thing for you to do is to be patient until an opportunity clearly reveals itself.

Avoid half-hearted investments. When you invest in something, be sure that there are good reasons to support your action, and you should feel good about your investment. Remember that you are not obliged to make any investment. But, when you do put your money in something, be as certain as possible that it is a profitable venture, like investing in Bitcoin.

You are not limited to applying only one strategy. In fact, many investors apply both fundamental analysis and technical analysis at the same time before making an investment. It is important that you have as much information as possible before you come up with an investment decision. This is the way to increase your chances of making a nice profit.

➢ Buy and hold

This is a common strategy used by beginners, but it is also one of the most effective strategies when you deal with bitcoins. In fact, many people who became millionaires with bitcoins used this simple strategy.

As the name suggests, the way this strategy works is simply to buy bitcoins, hold on to them for some time as you wait for the price of Bitcoin to increase, and then sell them for profit. Here is a classic example: Had you used this strategy even with just a $400 investment back in 2009 or 2010, then you would have been a multimillionaire by now. The simplicity of this strategy is what makes it very effective. There is no complicated research or analysis that you need to do. Just believe in the power of Bitcoin and put your money into it. Soon, you will reap your big reward. Is this strategy still applicable today? If you look at the past and present trend of Bitcoin, it is obvious that this is still one of the best strategies that you can use to earn a nice profit. As long as the price of Bitcoin keeps going up, you can make a profit. Hence, the earlier that you use this strategy, and as long as Bitcoin sticks to its increasing trend, then this simple strategy will earn you a nice positive profit over time.

➢ Averaging down

This is a good way to earn a huge amount of bitcoins. It will also allow you to purchase bitcoins at a "bargain." So, how does it work? The best way to explain how this works is by using an illustrative example: Let us say that the current price of bitcoin is $11,500. If its price drops to $11,450, you should make a buy order at the said lower amount. Now, if the price again decreases, let us say, down to $11,430, you make another buy order at $11,430. Now, let us assume that the price drops again to $11,400, then you should make another buy order at the said lower amount. *Wait a second; aren't you just buying a losing asset?* The answer is no. In fact, you are buying bitcoin at a bargain. The key to profit will hit once the price of bitcoin returns back to its original amount (its amount when you first applied this strategy), or higher, perhaps due to usual fluctuations in price or otherwise. When this happens, just imagine how much profit you can make. All the buy order that you have made will experience a nice profit.

➤ Quick sell

This is the opposite and a short version of averaging down strategy. When you use the quick sell strategy, you invest in bitcoins and sell for a profit as quickly as possible. You should be content with a small yet guaranteed profit. In order to get a decent amount of profit, you will have to invest a bigger amount since you will only target to earn even just 3% overall profit. Take note of the difference between the buy price and the sell price. Make sure to take it into account so that you will know the right amount at which to sell your bitcoins for a profit.

➤ Pump and dump

There is a reason why Bitcoin investors keep promoting Bitcoin. The principle is similar to a pump and dump activity that is usually used in stocks. The same applies to Bitcoin. The more that bitcoin draws attention and interest, the more likely that its price will increase. This is how its price also gets pumped these days, especially now that it has gained worldwide popularity and attention. Hence, the more that it is being promoted, the higher its price can get.

When you use trading platforms, you may notice that less known cryptocurrencies are being subject to a pump and dump scheme. Although this does not appear on the news, it is not uncommon for lesser known cryptocurrencies to experience more than 100% increase in value in just a week's time. Apparently, there are people who use the pump and dump scheme in cryptocurrencies.

Best Trading Practices

➤ Sufficient research

Many investors already engage in some form of study or research before making an investment. However, a common mistake is failing to do sufficient research. Do not think that just because you have spent several hours on the computer researching about Bitcoin or any other cryptocurrency that it would already be enough for you to make a wise investment decision. Make it a point to conduct as much in-depth research as possible. Fortunately, when you deal with Bitcoin, it is much easier to make a decision since the trend of Bitcoin these days clearly shows a positive sign that it is, indeed, a lucrative investment. Still, it is hard to tell the future. Therefore, you should make it a priority to always conduct a thorough research in order to help you come up with a wise investment/trading decision.

➤ Be updated on the news

When you deal with bitcoins, then the news is your number one source of information. When China declared that it will close down its local Bitcoin exchanges, it adversely affected the price of Bitcoin. However, when a news piece was featured on CNN about how profitable investing in bitcoins can be, it caused a further increase in the price of Bitcoin. When Russia declared that it would no longer outlaw the use of Bitcoin, and when Singapore declared that it will not impose any restriction upon the use of Bitcoin — these things were followed by an increase in the price of Bitcoin. As you can see, the news can reflect the direction that Bitcoin will take. Normally, if there is good news about Bitcoin, then its price will tend to increase;

however, if it is the contrary, then a decrease in price can be expected. By being updated on the news and analyzing what it says, you will be more able to come up with the right investment decision.

Another effective way to gain more information is by joining online groups and forums about Bitcoin and cryptocurrency in general. In fact, this is also an effective way to gain first-hand information since many cryptocurrency developers are active in online groups and forums. It is important for you to learn about the news on Bitcoin as early as possible in order to give you enough time to analyze it and make an appropriate response.

➢ Develop your own understanding

When you are a beginner, you will most likely rely on what "experts" publish on their blogs. Although this is good for beginners, you should know that it is important for you to soon develop your own understanding of bitcoin, including the whole cryptocurrency market in general. The reason is that many of these so-called "experts" are not as they claim to be. In today's world, it is easy to promote one's self as an expert in any field with just a few clicks of a mouse. The power and reach of social media and the use of advertisements can be used to deceive people. Sad to say, but many of these people who claim to be experts when it comes to Bitcoin and trading cryptocurrencies are not real experts. In fact, they probably have more losses than profits. Instead of completely relying on expert advice, you should treat their pieces of advice as they are: just mere "advice" or suggestions. It is also noteworthy that even the real cryptocurrency experts out there also commit mistakes from time to time. Therefore, it is important that you work on developing your own understanding and always take whatever you read or watch about bitcoins (or any other cryptocurrency) with a grain of salt.

➢ Use a trading journal

Having a trading journal is not something that you are required to do. In fact, there are many investors out there who have never had a trading journal in their life. However, using a trading journal can also be highly beneficial. Therefore, it is suggested that you write a trading journal for your Bitcoin adventure. A trading journal will allow you to view yourself from a different perspective and make you think outside the box. You can write anything that you want in your journal that is related to Bitcoin. Ideally, you should also write in your journal the strategies that you are using, as well as a record of your trades/investments.

When you use a journal, the important thing is to update it regularly and to be completely honest with everything that you write in it. Your trading journal will serve as a mirror of yourself as a Bitcoin investor/trader. It will allow you to think more clearly and even discover ways to improve your strategies. Overall, it will make you a better investor.

➢ Stay objective

Remember that no matter what happens in a trade or investment, you need to remain as objective as possible. Being an investor can be a lonely and isolated life. This is the kind of career where no one would care about you even if you lose all your investment money in one day. The Bitcoin market will not stop for you. It is not even slightly concerned about you. In fact, it does not even know that you exist. Therefore, do not let your emotions to cloud your judgment. Although having passion in what you do is good, allowing it to cloud your thinking can cause you to lose your investment. Remember to stay objective at all times. This also means thinking objectively.

➢ Diversify

"Do not put all your eggs in one basket." When dealing with something that is as volatile as Bitcoin, it is wise to spread your risk by diversifying. Do not go all in in one trade or investment. As stated in a previous chapter, you should not also keep all your bitcoins in one wallet. You should be prepared for contingencies. A good way to do this is by preparing for the worst. Learn to diversify your investments. However, take note that diversifying does not mean sacrificing the quality of your decisions. Every investment or trade that you make should always be backed up with sufficient study and analysis.

➢ Continuous practice

Although investing in Bitcoin can be as easy as using a buy and hold strategy, trading bitcoins with other cryptocurrencies effectively takes time and practice. If you are an active trader, then you should realize that the activity of trading takes so much more than reading books about cryptocurrency trading. You should also engage in actual practice. A good way to practice is by using the demo account that is usually provided by a trading broker. You may also choose to trade only small amounts when you are just starting out. If you are a new trader, then your first objective should be to familiarize yourself with actual process of trading and to develop an effective strategy. Do not focus on making profits right away. Once you have developed an effective strategy, then profits will follow.

➢ Take a break

The world of Bitcoin can be addicting. Some people get so obsessed with it that they spend their day doing almost nothing but reading books and watching videos about Bitcoin. However, you should remind yourself that taking a break is also important. If you give your body and mind enough time to just relax, then you will be more able to think and work for effectively. Therefore, give yourself the chance to relax from time to time, especially after a day's hard work. Also, when you take a rest, do something that will take your mind off of anything that is related to Bitcoin. Unfortunately, some people still think of Bitcoin when they rest. That is not the correct way to relax your mind. Do not worry; after that time for relaxation, you are expected to work on your investments more seriously and effectively.

Top 5 Mistakes to Avoid While Trading Bitcoin

➢ Lack of information

It is unfortunate that many investors do not understand what they are doing. If you want to make any investment, you should make it a priority to find out as much information as you can about the thing that you are investing in. For example, even though there is so much positive noise about Bitcoin today, you should not hurry to make an investment right away without learning and understanding what it really is. The fact that you are reading this book is a good sign that you want to be educated before you spend your heard-earned money. Unfortunately, there are people who get easily swayed and just go with the flow. The bad thing about this is that the "flow" does not always lead to a profitable position. When you invest in Bitcoin or deal with any other kind of cryptocurrency, be sure that you obtain as much information as possible. Needless to say, you should not make any investment or trade if you feel like you still need more details about something. Of course, the truth remains that despite the amount of information that you may gather, there is still no 100% guarantee that you will end up with a positive profit; however, keep in mind that the more information that you have, the more likely that you will be able to predict the direction that Bitcoin is going to take.

➢ Trading under pressure

Have you noticed how calm professional traders are even when they lose a trade or investment? True professional traders can control themselves even when under pressure. They have discipline and are able to maintain their composure even under stressful situations. The problem with trading under pressure is that it has a tendency to get your emotions in the way and cloud your judgment. Remember that you should be as objective as possible when you deal with Bitcoin or any other cryptocurrency. You cannot afford to be too emotional. In order to avoid trading under pressure, you should only invest the money that you can afford to lose. This means that you should not use the money that you need to pay for your household bills and other obligations. If you use the money that you need for your basic needs, then you will definitely be trading under pressure. The truth is that no amount of preparation can guarantee the success of any trade or investment. Therefore, it is never a good decision to make an investment using the money that you need for your necessities.

> Chasing after your losses

This is a very common mistake that is committed by so many people. A surprising thing about this is that those who commit it are actually aware of this teaching and yet they continue to violate this simple rule. The reason why this happens is because it is very tempting to chase after your losses, especially right after you experience a bad loss. For example, you might trade your bitcoins for another cryptocurrency and the value of the latter suddenly drops. If you experience a bad loss, say, a 30% loss, then you would be strongly tempted to chase after your losses. When a person chases after his losses, the tendency is to make a huge investment or trade and hope that it will end up profitably. The problem here is that such kind of investment is never guaranteed to end up in a profit. So, if you get unlucky and it fails, then you surely suffer a very bad loss.

Instead of chasing after your losses, what you should focus on is chasing after more profits. When you experience a loss, just accept that you have lost a transaction and then move on. Do not be too hard on yourself. After all, in the life of a professional trader, losses are bound to happen. The important thing is to end up with a positive profit once you sum up all your profits and losses altogether.

Another problem with chasing one's losses is that it adversely affects your strategy. Many professional traders are very conservative and only use 1%-2% of their total funds per trade. If you chase after your losses, you might be tempted to trade even as high as 50% or higher of your funds in one go. This sudden change in one's strategy can exhaust your funds. Although there is a chance that this strategy can work and give you a nice return, chances are that you will end up with a really bad loss in the long run if you keep on chasing after your losses.

➢ Greed

Greed is another thing that you should watch out for. Although it is good to desire to have more profit, it is not good to get too greedy to make a profit. When you invest in Bitcoin, there is already a high chance that you will make a profit if you are patient enough. Here is a real-life example of how greed can ruin your investment. I know someone who invests in Bitcoin professionally. For a few years, he enjoyed lots of slow but steady profit by investing in Bitcoin. One day, he learned about trading cryptocurrencies and the beauty (or danger) or margin trading, where you can trade an additional 60% or so of your total funds. He made lots of profit in the first few weeks. After a few more days, he experienced a bad loss, so he chased after his losses, and then ended up with only 30% of his original investment remaining in his trading account. This means that he had lost all profits, as well as 70% of his total investment. Had he not been greedy and just stuck to the steady gains with mere Bitcoin investing, he would have been a multimillionaire by now. So, once again, always remember: Do not be greedy.

➢ Using an untested strategy

There are many strategies that you can use when you invest in or trade bitcoins. If you trade different kinds of cryptocurrencies, then you will definitely be learning more strategies than the usual ones. Now, you should keep in mind that you must always test your strategy before you use it with a real investment. Take note that even if you just make a minor modification in your strategy, you must still test it several times. The reason is that strategies are very sensitive. What you think as a minor adjustment can have a major effect upon its effectiveness. A good way to test your strategy is by using the demo account provided by your trading broker, if any, or simply trade using a small amount just to see if it will work or not.

What to Look for in a Trading Platform

➢ Latest reviews

Before you engage in trading, you will need to create an account with a trading platform. There are many sites online that will allow you to trade bitcoins and other cryptocurrencies. You should always check the latest reviews before using a particular trading platform. Also pay attention to the dates when the last reviews were made. It is also not uncommon for trading brokers to hire freelance writers to come up with a positive write-up about their platform, so do not rely on a single website when looking for reviews. The more reviews that you read from different websites, the better.

> ➢ Responsive customer support

When you trade professionally, there may come a time when you will have to contact the site's support team to ask a question. You will find this helpful, especially if you notice a bug in the site or in case of technical problems. Therefore, it is important that you use a trading platform that has active customer support. The best way to find out just how reliable the customer support is of a particular platform is by testing it. Even before you make any deposit, try sending a message to the site's customer support. Inquire about something and see how quickly and professionally the customer support team handles your inquiry.

> ➢ Platform design and layout

Although the design and layout of a trading platform is not of primary importance, it will still be beneficial if the platform is professionally designed. It will set you in the right mood for trading. Also, the site should be easy to navigate. You should be able to buy, sell, and trade bitcoins easily with just a few clicks of a mouse. A simple yet professional layout is preferred in order to avoid confusion.

> ➢ Mobile feature

These days, the easiest way to access the Internet is through your mobile phone. Your trading platform should allow you to access and manage your account completely from your mobile device. You should also be able to buy and sell bitcoins (or other cryptocurrencies) simply through your mobile phone. Being able to access the platform through your mobile phone is not enough. The experience should also be easy and convenient. Do not worry; most reliable platforms recognize the importance of a mobile feature and make sure that their site offers a decent mobile version of the trading platform.

➤ Trading tools

Your trading platform should provide you with tools that can help you make a sound investment decision. This is important especially if you are into technical analysis. Ideally, you should be provided with updated graphs that show the price behavior of a particular cryptocurrency.

➤ Margin trading

One of the reasons why many investors like to trade cryptocurrency is because of margin trading. Margin trading is where you can borrow cryptocurrency from your broker of up to more than around 60% or even 75% (or even higher) of your total funds. This will allow you to make more trades, which would mean a higher profit potential. Of course, you should also pay attention to the margin call or the time when you are supposed to pay interest to your broker. If you are a beginner, it is not advised to do margin trading. Although margin trading can be very tempting to do, beginners are well advised to avoid it and just focus on developing an effective strategy.

➤ Withdrawal requirements and processing

It is not uncommon for a trading broker to request for certain documents before it starts to process a withdrawal, especially if it is your first time to request a withdrawal. Before you deposit any cryptocurrency in your account, make sure that you know the requirements of your broker for making a withdrawal and that you have these documents available in your possession. Normally, the required documents would be valid ID's and a statement of account with your billing address. It is noteworthy that some brokers would not require you to submit such documents and would simply respect your anonymity. If you are withdrawing a big amount, then you can expect for your broker to request you to submit such documents before it processes your withdrawal. Also take note of how many days it will take for your broker to complete a withdrawal request. Ideally, all withdrawal requests should be processed and completed within 24 hours.

How to become a Millionaire in Trading Bitcoin and Cryptocurrency

➢ Erik Finman

Mr. Finman made a bet with his parents that if he became a millionaire by the time he reached 18, his parents would not force him to go to college. Thanks to his investment in Bitcoin, Mr. Finman is now a multimillionaire. "I can proudly say I made it," Finman said, "and I'm not going to college."

➢ Jeremy Gardner

Mr. Gardner dropped out of college and only worked part-time at a venture capital firm. He also tried making a fortune by investing in stocks. However, it did not turn out to be as profitable as he had expected. Today, Jeremy Gardner travels the world as a multimillionaire. He was one of the people who spotted the great potential of Bitcoin. He sold all his stock holdings and switched all his investments to Bitcoin cryptocurrency. It was the best investment move that he had ever done.

➢ Gavin Andersen

Rumor has it that Mr. Andersen is Satoshi Nakamoto; however, it is something that Mr. Andersen denies. He claims that he closely corresponded with Mr. Nakamoto. He also maintains Bitcoin's source code, so no wonder he will be a big success. Today, he is a multimillionaire. Once again, all this is possible because of Bitcoin.

➢ Olaf-Carlson Wee

26-year old Olaf-Carlson Wee worked at Coinbase, a popular Bitcoin web wallet, back in February 2013. Even at that time, he claimed to have already known the big potential of Bitcoin, and so he decided to receive his salary in bitcoins. At that time, Bitcoin was only worth around $25. Today, Olaf is a multimillionaire and believes that Bitcoin is a more democratic type of currency. As much as possible, he uses bitcoins in his transactions.

➢ Kristoffer Koch

He bought 5,000 bitcoins in 2009 using 150 kroner. At that time, the investment was only worth $26.60. Around the same time, he was also writing a thesis about encryption. It was then when he came across Bitcoin and decided to give it a try. After buying 5,000 bitcoins, he completely forgot about them. It was only in 2013 when he remembered his investment in Bitcoin because of the media coverage. He remembered storing his Bitcoin in an e-wallet but could not remember the password. Fortunately, after numerous attempts, he was able to access his Bitcoin wallet. To his surprise, he found $886,000 worth of bitcoins.

➤ Erik Finman

Back in 2012, Erik Finman, who was only 15 at that time, had the motivation to make an investment. One Easter, he received $1,000 from his grandmother as a gift. He used it all to purchase bitcoins. A year after this incident, the value of his bitcoins rose to $100,000. He then sold all his bitcoins for a profit. Today, he runs a video tutoring service company and pays all his employees using bitcoins.

This list is much less than the tip of the iceberg. There are so many people who have earned a fortune by investing in Bitcoin. The good news is that even to this day, more and more people are continuously making money with Bitcoin. Yes, you read that right — Bitcoin is still a lucrative investment. If you want to join the list of highly successful people, then now is the time to take advantage of what Bitcoin offers.

Bitcoin Mining

Mining bitcoins is another way to earn bitcoins. In fact, this activity used to be a very popular way to earn bitcoins. Generally, there are four ways to mine for bitcoins: Computer mining, hardware mining, software mining, and cloud mining.

➤ Computer mining

Did you know that you can mine bitcoins using your own computer? You can use a GUI miner to do it. You simply have to connect to a mining pool, and you can start earning bitcoins. Is it really that easy? The answer is *no*. Mining using your own computer alone will make you end up with more expenses than profit. You will most likely spend more on your electric bill than the amount of bitcoins you can earn. If you just want to test and experience how bitcoin mining works, then you can try to mine using your own computer. However, do not expect to earn a decent amount of bitcoins from this activity. Also, be careful not to overheat your computer. If you just use your computer, you may barely get even just 0.000003 bitcoins for a whole day of mining. It is simply not worth it. The problem here is that a home computer does not have enough hash power to mine more bitcoins. In order to get more hash power, you will have to use hardware in addition to your computer, which leads us to the next topic.

➢ Hardware mining

Hardware mining is where you mine bitcoins using your computer and mining hardware. The hardware will give you more hash power that you need to mine more bitcoins. Now, the drawback with using hardware mining is that you will have to purchase mining hardware, which can be costly. Needless to say, it is not a good idea to invest in a cheap mining hardware. Another issue with hardware mining is overheating. Since you will be mining bitcoins for hours, this means that you will have to use your computer and mining hardware also for hours regularly. In the long run, this can break your computer, as well as your mining hardware. Hence, when you use this approach, be sure to follow a schedule and avoid overheating your computer and hardware.

➢ Software mining

There are companies that sell mining software. All that you need to do is to download and install that software in your computer and use it to mine for bitcoins. The problem with this approach is that you will have to purchase software. Many times, the software that is being promoted is not really good enough to allow you to mine a decent amount of bitcoins, much less to recover what you have paid to buy the software. You also have to worry about overheating, since you will still be using your computer for mining. Not to mention, there are also scammers out there who sell software that will not do its job well. So, be careful where you buy your mining software.

➢ Cloud mining

Cloud mining is the most popular way to mine bitcoins these days. With cloud mining, you do not have to worry about having any issue with overheating. When you do cloud mining, a mining company that has powerful hardware will do all the mining work for you. All that you need to do is wait for the mining company to send you your bitcoins. Usually, the bitcoins will be sent on a weekly or monthly basis, or even immediately once you reach the minimum threshold for payout. So, is there any drawback? Although cloud mining appears to be the most recommended way to mine for bitcoins, there are some things that you should pay attention to. When you use cloud mining, you will have to pay a certain amount to a mining company before it starts to mine for you. Of course, this is only fair. A typical offer may look something like this: Pay/deposit 1 bitcoin and get 0.03 bitcoins every week. Although this may look like a good offer, the problem is that what the mining company shows you is only the *expected* return, and not the actual return that you will receive. Hence, even if the offer states that you will earn 0.03 bitcoin every week, you may only receive 0.02 or even less. Therefore, before you even deposit any money, be sure to read the terms and conditions of the contract.

When you work with a mining company, it may offer you to purchase more miners or hashes. The purpose of this is to increase the amount of bitcoins that you will receive. The more hashes or miners you have, the more bitcoins you can earn. It is advised that before you make use of this feature, you should first check if you are dealing with a legitimate mining company. Have you made any successful withdrawals recently? If you have not made any withdrawal yet, then try to spend as little as possible. Unfortunately, there have been many reports online where people do not receive payments from mining companies. This is another serious problem when you do cloud mining. It is not something that is within your control. You rely solely on the mining company. Hence, if the mining company suddenly chooses not to pay you, then things can get complicated.

When you buy a miner or more hash power, you should check for the expiry date. Many cloud mining companies will allow you to purchase and use miners or hash power for a limited amount of time, usually for about a year or a few months. Once the time expires, then you will have to make another purchase. Before you consider this option, you need to compute if you will really end up with a positive profit.

You should only work with trusted and reliable cloud mining companies. Hence, you should do your research and check the latest reviews and ratings of a mining company before you make any deposit/payment.

Although cloud mining can still be profitable, especially in the long run, many experts suggest that if you are really serious about making money with Bitcoin, then the best way is to learn how to invest/trade bitcoins effectively.

Chapter 5:

The Future of Bitcoin

The Future of Bitcoin and the Challenges It Faces

B itcoin was once imagined as the future of money. Today, that future has already arrived. Bitcoin is revolutionizing the world and making positive and significant changes. If you examine the past and current trend of Bitcoin, it is easy to see the growing demand for this cryptocurrency, as well as its constantly increasing value. With all the good things going on with Bitcoin, are there still challenges that it is facing? The answer would be in the affirmative. Just like any other successful technology or innovation, Bitcoin also faces some challenges. The risks that have always been in the nature of Bitcoin have followed it even to its success. This means that it is still vulnerable to market risk, legal risk, security rick, and technological risk, among others. With the popularity that Bitcoin has reached, it has also drawn the attention and concern of the government. In the future, it is expected that Bitcoin will be more closely monitored and regulated by governments. Although as of the present time it seems that only a few governments impose restrictions on Bitcoin, it does not mean that governments will just stand idle months or years from now. After all, Bitcoin also poses a threat to the financial industry, especially in the banking industry.

Is Bitcoin just another bubble? This is the question that people has been asking for years already. However, if you look at it closely, it appears that Bitcoin is for real. In the past, many experts already confirmed that Bitcoin was a bubble that was about to burst at any time. But look at Bitcoin today, and you can say that those "experts" were wrong. In fact, Bitcoin is gaining more followers, and it is getting stronger and stronger. Quite surprisingly, big companies and even governments from different parts of the world are now supporting Bitcoin. Indeed, despite the many challenges that Bitcoin has faced and will still be facing, it has proven that it can withstand the test of time and is here to stay.

Of course, there is still a possibility that Bitcoin might totally disappear in the near future, just as there is a possibility for banks and other institutions to just vanish out of thin air. However, a close look at the direction of Bitcoin would easily make anyone realize that it is not a bubble that will just burst into nothingness. Rather, it is a revolution that the world needs. Bitcoin is the new culture.

How Bitcoin Can and Will Disrupt the Financial System

As you already know, Bitcoin is not just a lucrative investment; it is also a substitute for money and a payment system. The threat of Bitcoin to soon take the place of banks and other financial institutions is more real and probable than you might think. Experts have already proven that indeed Bitcoin can be an effective substitute not only for money, but that it can also take the place of banks. What is more, it will be able to lower down costs and make much faster transactions. This is because Bitcoin is not just a cryptocurrency; it is also powered by blockchain, which is also a revolutionizing technology. In fact, studies show that blockchain technology can be used for accounting purposes, bookkeeping, notarial service, recordings, supply-chain management, and others. And, of course, it can also take the place of banks.

It is not really about Bitcoin disrupting the financial system; rather, Bitcoin will most probably be the financial system. To date, there is no other system that can match what Bitcoin offers. The only thing that is needed is for people to be more open to the idea of using it. Judging the trend of Bitcoin, it can be said that Bitcoin is well on its way to ruling the financial sector in the world.

Bitcoin: The One-World (Crypto)Currency

For years, there have been rumors of a one-world currency that will be used, recognized, and respected throughout the world. Today, it seems clear that the said prophecy refers to Bitcoin. Bitcoin has gained and is continuously gaining worldwide use and acceptance. Every day the number of people who own bitcoins is increasing. In our modern era, this is also the time when people love to make transactions online. After all, why bother to leave the comfort of your home when you can make transactions with just a few clicks of a mouse or directly through your mobile phone? Of course, this is something that Bitcoin is really good at. In fact, it is made for this purpose, that it exists completely online to serve your needs. It is just a matter of time before Bitcoin can be recognized as the one-world (crypto)currency. As of today, it is already doing its job and is in the right direction. With more support coming from individuals, merchants, companies, and even governments, Bitcoin is definitely going to rule the world. Indeed, this cryptocurrency is the new modern revolution that is reshaping the world like never before. This 2018 is the perfect time for a change. It is the time for you to make a difference. It is the time of Bitcoin.

Conclusion

Thanks for making it through to the end of this book. We hope it was informative and able to provide you with all of the tools you need to achieve your goals, whatever they may be.

The next step is to apply everything that you have learned. So start investing in Bitcoin today and make your way to financial freedom.

Indeed, Bitcoin is the new revolution. In order to get the most benefit, you should take advantage of it as early as possible. This is not about placing pressure on you to buy bitcoins, but the truth is that its price is now constantly increasing. Each day that you delay taking the right actions is like losing another percentage of profit.

By now you should have already realized that Bitcoin is the real deal. If you think that $11,000 for 1 Bitcoin is already good enough, then wait and watch how Bitcoin will surprise the world this 2018. It is fair to say that Bitcoin is still a young technology. As experts suggest, this 2018, Bitcoin will reach even more than $30,000. This is just the beginning for Bitcoin. It is not a bubble that is about to burst. It is a bubble that will conquer the world.

www.ingramcontent.com/pod-product-compliance
Lightning Source LLC
Chambersburg PA
CBHW070515220526
45467CB00002B/667